THE ULTIMATE BROOKLYN NETS BOOK FOR KIDS AND TEENS

160+ Fun, Surprising, And Educational Stories And Trivia Quizzes About Players And History

John Stevenson

First published 2025

Copyright © John Stevenson, 2025

All rights reserved. No part of this book may be used or reproduced in any manner whatsoever without written permission except in the case of brief quotations embodied in articles and reviews.

ISBN 9798313436722

Contents

CHAPTER ONE: The Beginning: Brooklyn Nets Early Years — 6

CHAPTER TWO: Famous Rivalries — 12

CHAPTER THREE: Legendary Players — 21

Julius Erving — 22
Buck Williams — 26
Dražen Petrović — 30
Jason Kidd — 34
Vince Carter — 39
Brook Lopez — 44
Joe Johnson — 48

Kevin Durant   52

CHAPTER FOUR: Coaches And Their Impact   71

CHAPTER FIVE: Memorable Moments in Nets History: Wins, Historic Games, And Record-Breaking Performances   79

CHAPTER SIX: Fun Facts and Trivia   92

BONUS QUIZ! More Brooklyn Nets Questions! 97

CHAPTER ONE
The Beginning: Brooklyn Nets Early Years

The Brooklyn Nets started in 1967 as the New Jersey Americans in the ABA (American Basketball Association). Their first season was rough. They tied for the last playoff spot but had to forfeit because their court was in bad shape.

In 1968, they moved to Long Island and became the New York Nets. The name "Nets" was chosen because it rhymed with the Mets and the Jets.

The team struggled at first. In the 1968-69 season, they won only 17 games and had small crowds at games. Some had fewer than 400 fans.

Things got better in 1970 when they got Rick Barry, a star player. He helped them reach the ABA Finals in 1972, but they lost to the Indiana Pacers. After Barry left, the team had to rebuild again.

In 1973, the Nets signed Julius Erving, also known as "Dr. J." He was an amazing player and made the team great. In 1974, the Nets won 55 games and their first ABA Championship by beating the Utah Stars. Erving was named the Most Valuable Player.

In 1976, Erving led the Nets to another 55-win season. The Nets won the last ABA championship, defeating the Denver Nuggets.

That year, the ABA and NBA merged. The Nets joined the NBA, but it was not easy. They had to pay a lot of money to enter the league. On top of that, they had to pay the New York Knicks millions for playing in their area.

The team had no money left. To fix this, they sold their best player, Julius Erving, to the Philadelphia 76ers. Losing Dr. J was a disaster. The team went from being a champion to one of the worst in the NBA.

Their first NBA season (1976-77) was awful. They won only 22 games and lost 60. Fans were unhappy, and things got worse. After just one year in the NBA, the team moved back to New Jersey in 1977. They became the New Jersey Nets.

Even in New Jersey, the team kept losing. They missed the playoffs for years. In 1981, they drafted Buck Williams, a strong rebounder. He helped the team improve. In 1982-83, they finally made the playoffs but lost in the first round.

Things changed in the early 2000s when the Nets traded for Jason Kidd. Kidd was a fantastic point guard, and he turned the Nets into a winning team.

The Nets made the NBA Finals in 2002 and 2003, but they lost both times. Even though they didn't win, this was one of the best times in team history.

In 2012, the team moved to Brooklyn and became the Brooklyn Nets. In 2019, the Nets made big moves. They signed Kevin Durant and Kyrie Irving, two of the best players in the NBA.

Later, they added James Harden, forming one of the most talented teams in NBA history. Many thought they would win a championship. But, injuries, drama, and team problems stopped them. Harden left in 2022, and both Durant and Irving were traded in 2023.

The Brooklyn Nets have had good times and bad times. They have been through tough losses and great victories. No matter what, they have always been a team that represents the hardworking spirit of Brooklyn.

CHAPTER ONE QUIZ

1. What year were the Nets founded?

a. 1967

b. 1970

c. 1973

d. 1978

2. How many games did the Nets win in the 1968-69 season?

a. 12 games

b. 17 games

c. 39 games

d. 55 games

3. What was the original name of the team in 1967?

a. New Jersey Knicks

b. New Jersey Nets

c. New Jersey Islanders

d. New Jersey Americans

4. Which star player did the Nets draft in 1970?

a. Julius Erving

b. Buck Williams

c. Rick Barry

d. Jason Kidd

5. Which year did the Nets win their first ABA Championship?

a. 1971

b. 1974

c. 1975

d. 1977

6. Which team did the Nets defeat in the 1976 ABA Championship?

a. Denver Nuggets

b. Golden State Warriors

c. Philadelphia 76ers

d. Indiana Pacers

7. Which year did the Nets move to Brooklyn and became the Brooklyn Nets?

a. 2006

b. 2019

c. 2011

d. 2012

Quiz Answers

1. 1967 **2.** 17 games **3.** New Jersey Americans **4.** Rick Barry **5.** 1974 **6.** Denver Nuggets **7.** 2012

CHAPTER TWO
Famous Rivalries

As the Brooklyn Nets became one of the most popular NBA teams, many major rivals look to defeat the Nets every time they meet.

Here are three of the Nets' fiercest rivals, whose intense matchups have produced some of the most exciting and memorable moments in NBA history.

New York Knicks

The Brooklyn Nets and the New York Knicks have a rivalry that is all about New York City basketball. Both teams play in the same city, and their fans argue about which team represents New York. The Knicks have been around much longer, but the Nets have worked hard to make their mark.

The rivalry started when the Nets joined the NBA in 1976 after playing in a different league, the ABA. Back then, the Knicks were already a legendary team with two championships. Meanwhile, the Nets were still trying to find their place.

For a long time, the Knicks were the more popular team. But, everything changed when the Nets moved from New Jersey to Brooklyn in 2012.

In 2012, the Nets got new colors, a new logo, and a fresh start in Brooklyn. Both teams were now battling for New York's basketball fans.

The Nets built a strong team with Deron Williams, Joe Johnson, Paul Pierce, and Kevin Garnett. Meanwhile, the Knicks had Carmelo Anthony leading the way. Their games were heated, and fans filled the arenas with energy every time they played.

One of the most exciting moments in this rivalry came in 2022. Kevin Durant and Kyrie Irving led the Nets. They went on a nine-game winning streak against the Knicks.

The Nets dominated the rivalry during that time. They showed that Brooklyn was a serious basketball city.

Every time these teams meet, it's a battle. The battle for New York basketball is still going strong, and the rivalry will only get bigger in the future.

Boston Celtics

The Brooklyn Nets and the Boston Celtics have built a strong rivalry. The rivalry is filled with playoff battles, superstar trades, and intense matchups.

The Celtics have one of the most successful histories in basketball. Meanwhile, the Nets have fought to make their mark, especially after moving to Brooklyn in 2012.

The rivalry became really heated in 2013 when the Nets made a huge trade with the Celtics. The Nets traded for Paul Pierce, Kevin Garnett, and Jason Terry. They were three former Celtics stars, and the Nets hoped they would help win a championship.

But the plan didn't work out and the Nets continued to struggle. The Celtics used the draft picks they got in the trade to rebuild. They drafted young stars like Jayson Tatum and Jaylen Brown. This made Boston stronger while the Nets had to start over.

In 2021, the rivalry got even bigger when the teams met in the NBA Playoffs. The games were even more intense because of Kyrie Irving. Irving used to play for Boston. After he joined the Nets, he had a lot of tension with Celtics fans.

The Nets had a superstar trio of Irving, Kevin Durant, and James Harden. They easily beat the Celtics in the first round, 4-1.

But in 2022, the Celtics swept the Nets 4-0 in the playoffs, completely shutting them down.

The rivalry is still strong between the Nets and the Celtics. Each game is a chance to prove who is the better team. Whenever both teams play, it feels personal.

Toronto Raptors

While the Raptors are Canada's only NBA team, the Nets have been their toughest opponent in some of their biggest games.

The rivalry started getting serious in 2004 when the Nets traded for Vince Carter. He had been Toronto's biggest star.

Raptors fans were upset because Carter had been their best player, and now he was playing for a rival team. Every time he visited Toronto, he got booed and double-teamed whenever he touched the ball.

However, the two teams did not meet in the playoffs until 2007, when the Nets defeated the Raptors, 4–2. The rivalry started to die down after Vince Carter left the Nets during the 2009 offseason.

In 2014, the teams met again in the first round. The Nets and Raptors faced off in a tough first-round series that went to a Game 7 in Toronto.

With just seconds left, the Raptors had the ball and a chance to win. But, Paul Pierce blocked the final shot, helping the Nets win the series. It was a heartbreaking loss for Toronto.

The two teams met again in the 2020 NBA Playoffs, but this time the Raptors were the stronger team. Toronto swept the Nets 4-0, getting revenge for the 2014 loss.

Over the years, the rivalry has had big stars, close games, and plenty of drama. Whenever Brooklyn and Toronto play, there is always extra energy on the court.

CHAPTER TWO QUIZ

1. What started the rivalry between the Nets and Knicks?

a. The Nets defeated the Knicks in the ABA Championship

b. Both teams compete to be the best team in New York City

c. The Nets traded their best players to the Knicks

d. The Knicks defeated the Nets in the NBA Finals

2. How long was the Nets' winning streak against the Knicks in 2022?

a. 5 games

b. 7 games

c. 9 games

d. 11 games

3. What was the score when the Nets beat the Celtics in the 2021 playoffs?

a. 4-0

b. 4-1

c. 5-2

d. 5-1

4. Which year did the Nets and Raptors meet in the playoffs for the first time?

a. 2004

b. 2005

c. 2006

d. 2007

Quiz Answers

1. Both teams compete to be the best team in New York City **2.** 9 games **3.** 4-1 **4.** 2007

CHAPTER THREE
Legendary Players

The Nets have some of the greatest players to ever step onto a basketball court. Since the beginning of the NBA, the Nets have produced several Hall of Famers.

These famous Nets players have shown what it means to play for the Nets, whether they are winning a title or making amazing dunks.

JULIUS ERVING

NBA CHAMPION (1983)

2X ABA CHAMPION

11X NBA ALL-STAR

5X ALL-NBA FIRST TEAM

NBA MVP (1981)

BORN
February 22, 1950
East Meadow, New York, U.S.

POSITION
Small forward

NBA DRAFT
1972 / round: 1 / pick: 12

Julius Erving, also known as "Dr. J," is considered one of the greatest and most influential basketball players of all time. He could do it all. He could jump, run, shoot, score, dunk, play defense, and rebound.

His exciting dunks and smooth style helped change how the game was played. Julius was named to the All-NBA Team seven times. He won the NBA MVP Award in 1981 and led the 76ers to an NBA championship in the 1982-83 season.

Julius first earned the nickname "Dr. J" in high school. He showed flashes of his incredible talent there. Despite being a great player, he wasn't recruited by many big basketball programs.

Instead, he attended the University of Massachusetts. Julius dominated in college, averaging an amazing 32.5 points and 20.2 rebounds per game.

One afternoon, Julius sat in the cafeteria with his teammate, Artie. They were discussing the game from the night before.

"Man, Jules," Artie said, shaking his head. "Thirty points, fifteen rebounds, and that dunk in the second half? You're on another level."

Julius smiled. "Thanks, Artie. But you know, it's not just me. I've got great teammates like you setting me up."

"Yeah, yeah, I get that," Artie said. "But don't act like you're not out there doing magic. Do you ever think about what's next? You're tearing it up here, but what about the pros?"

Julius paused, taking a sip of his drink.

"Honestly? I'm just focused on getting better. The rest will take care of itself. But if I get a shot at the pros, you'd better believe I'll be ready."

Artie grinned. "Oh, I believe it. And when you're throwing down dunks on TV, remember who called it first."

Julius left college before his senior year to turn professional in 1971. He joined the Virginia Squires, a team in the American Basketball Association (ABA).

In his rookie season, he averaged over 27 points per game. But his career took off when he moved to the New York Nets in 1973.

With the Nets, Julius led the team to ABA championships in 1974 and 1976. He was named the league's Most Valuable Player in both seasons.

Julius became famous for his incredible midair moves. He would spin and dunk with power. His high-flying style made him a fan favorite and helped make the ABA more exciting to watch.

In his five ABA seasons, Julius won two championships, three MVP awards, and three scoring titles. When the ABA merged with the NBA in 1976, Julius joined the Philadelphia 76ers.

Julius retired in 1987 at the age of 37, after playing 11 seasons with the 76ers. Over his career, combining both his ABA and NBA stats, he scored more than 30,000 points.

After retiring, Julius received many honors. He was named to the NBA's 50th Anniversary All-Time Team. In 1993, he was inducted into the Basketball Hall of Fame.

BUCK WILLIAMS

3X NBA ALL-STAR

1X ALL-NBA SECOND TEAM

2X NBA ALL-DEFENSIVE FIRST TEAM

BORN
March 8, 1960
Rocky Mount, North Carolina, U.S.

POSITION
Power forward

NBA DRAFT
1981 / round: 1 / pick: 3

Charles Linwood "Buck" Williams was one of the first big stars for the New Jersey Nets. He was an amazing rebounder and led the team in rebounding for most of the 1980s.

Buck grew up learning the importance of hard work. As a baby, he rode in a sack his mother carried while she picked cotton in North Carolina. His father worked long hours in construction.

Buck became a star player at the University of Maryland. He was named one of the best players in the ACC twice and was even picked for the 1980 USA Olympic basketball team.

One day, after Buck made his first big play in college, he remembered a conversation with his father.

"You've got to work for everything you want, son," Moses had told him when Buck was just starting school in Maryland. "Nothing will be handed to you. If you want to be the best, you've got to be relentless."

After three years in college, Buck decided to enter the NBA. The Nets picked him third overall in the 1981 NBA Draft.

Buck sat in the locker room before his first official game with the Nets. He was nervous, but his teammate, Albert King, noticed and approached him.

"You good, rookie?" King asked, noticing Buck fidgeting with his jersey.

Buck looked up, a slight smile on his face. "Yeah, just the usual pre-game nerves."

King chuckled. "I hear you. Just remember, it's just basketball. We're all here to play our part. You've already shown you can handle it. You've got this."

In his first season, he averaged 15.5 points and led the team with 12.3 rebounds per game. He helped the Nets win 20 more games than the year before. He was named the 1982 NBA Rookie of the Year.

When the news broke that Buck had won Rookie of the Year, the locker room was buzzing. His teammates surrounded him, congratulating him with claps on the back.

"You did it, Buck!" King shouted.

Buck smiled, holding up the trophy. "It's not just me. It's this whole team."

But the look in Buck's eyes told a different story. He knew that his work ethic and his will to succeed had brought him here.

For the next eight seasons, Buck was one of the best power forwards in the NBA. Six times, he was ranked among the top three rebounders in the league. He was always averaging more than 12 rebounds per game.

In the 1983-84 season, Buck helped the Nets reach the second round of the playoffs for the first time since 1976. He also made the All-Star team three times while playing for the

Nets. When he left the team, he was their all-time leader in total rebounds.

In 1989, the Nets traded Buck to the Portland Trail Blazers. He played there for seven seasons before joining the New York Knicks in 1996.

Buck retired in 1999 with career averages of 12.8 points and 10 rebounds per game. Over his 17-year NBA career, he scored more than 16,000 points and grabbed over 13,000 rebounds. He became just the seventh NBA player to reach both marks.

DRAŽEN PETROVIĆ

1X ALL-NBA THIRD TEAM

2X EUROLEAGUE CHAMPION

2X CROATIAN SPORTSMAN OF THE YEAR

BORN
22 October 1964
Šibenik, Croatia

POSITION
Shooting guard

NBA DRAFT
1986 / round: 3 / pick: 60

Dražen Petrović was a guard for the New Jersey Nets in the early 1990s and one of the best shooters ever. He was also one of the first international stars in the NBA.

Dražen grew up in Šibenik, a small port city by the Adriatic Sea. His father was a police chief. He and his brother, Aleksander, spent hours playing basketball on makeshift courts.

One afternoon, Aleksander wiped the sweat from his forehead. They had spent hours practicing in the hot sun. He watched Dražen dribble between his legs before launching a perfect shot.

"Dražen," Aleksander panted, still catching his breath, "do you ever stop? We've been out here for hours."

Dražen picked up the ball and spun it in his hands.

"And? One day, we're both going to play in the NBA. But only if we outwork everyone else."

Aleksander nodded, his competitive fire matching his brother's.

"Then we have to push each other. No excuses."

Dražen bounced the ball toward him.

"No excuses. The first one to miss ten shots has to run sprints."

By age 15, Dražen was already talented enough to join the Yugoslavian national team. The Portland Trail Blazers picked him in the third round of the 1986 NBA Draft.

31

But because of Yugoslavia's travel rules and his contract, he couldn't come to America right away. Instead, he played in Europe for Real Madrid in Spain, where he became a star.

Dražen finally joined the Blazers for the 1989–90 season. But, he didn't get much playing time. In 1991, he was traded to the Nets.

At first, the Nets did not play him much, but he became a starter by the 1991–92 season. He quickly became one of the best shooting guards in the NBA. He was known for scoring three-pointers.

In just four NBA seasons, Dražen made a huge impact with his energy and shooting skills. He averaged 21.4 points per game in his two full seasons with the Nets. His best season was in 1992–93 when he led the team with 22.3 points per game.

Sadly, his career was cut short when he died in a car accident in Germany. He was only 28 years old.

During his time with the Nets, he averaged 19.5 points, 2.8 rebounds, 2.9 assists, and 1.2 steals per game. In 2002, he was honored by being inducted into the Naismith Memorial Basketball Hall of Fame.

JASON KIDD

NBA CHAMPION (2011)

10X NBA ALL-STAR

5X ALL-NBA FIRST TEAM

4X NBA ALL-DEFENSIVE FIRST TEAM

BORN
March 23, 1973
San Francisco, California, U.S.

POSITION
Point guard

NBA DRAFT
1994 / round: 1 / pick: 2

Jason Kidd is one of the best players to ever wear a Nets uniform. He was one of the greatest point guards in NBA history, known for his amazing passing and court vision. He is second all-time in both assists and steals. He helped lead the Nets close to an NBA championship.

Jason was a star in high school. He won the Naismith Award as the best high school player in the country and was named Player of the Year twice. He was also California Player of the Year two times.

After one of his high school games, his coach pulled him aside in the locker room.

"You controlled the game tonight, Jason," his coach said, patting him on the shoulder.

Jason, still catching his breath, nodded.

"Thanks, Coach. I just try to keep everyone involved. It's not about me. It's about winning."

"That's why you're going to be great," his coach said. "You make your teammates better. Remember that. Scorers come and go, but guys like you, the playmakers, are the ones who change the game."

Many colleges wanted him, but he chose to play at the University of California, Berkeley. He helped make their basketball team great again. He broke records and became one of the best college players.

The Dallas Mavericks picked Jason with the second overall pick in the 1994 NBA Draft.

As a rookie, he averaged 11.7 points, 5.4 rebounds, and 7.7 assists. He also led the league in triple-doubles. Because of his great play, he won NBA Rookie of the Year, sharing the award with Grant Hill.

From 1996 to 2001, Jason played for the Phoenix Suns. He led them to the playoffs every season. In 2001, Jason was traded to the New Jersey Nets. He was already a star, but he became a legend with the Nets.

On his first day in practice with the Nets, Kenyon Martin walked up to him.

"You really think we can win here?"

Jason looked around at his new teammates.

"We don't have to think about winning," he said. "We just have to play with our hearts. And if we do that, the wins will come."

In his first season with the team, he helped them finish with a 52-30 record. The year before, they had only won 26 games.

Jason took them to the playoffs yearly in his seven seasons with the Nets and won the Atlantic Division four times. He also led them to two straight NBA Finals in 2002 and 2003.

After a tough playoff game, coach Byron Scott pulled Jason aside.

"You carried us again, but we need that one last push."

Jason wiped his face with a towel. "I know. We're close, Coach. One or two plays can change everything."

Scott nodded. "Then let's go make those plays."

Jason was a great passer and rebounder, always a threat to get a triple-double. He was not the biggest, strongest, or fastest player, but he was smart and knew hows to control the game.

He also hustled for every loose ball, grabbing 3,662 rebounds in his career, which is rare for a 6'4" guard.

In a sport where scoring is often the most important thing, Jason made passing exciting. He made his teammates better and had fun doing it.

In 2008, Jason was traded back to Dallas. He finished his playing career in 2013 with the New York Knicks.

He won an NBA championship with the Dallas Mavericks in 2011 and also won two Olympic gold medals with Team USA in 2000 and 2008.

In 2018, Jason Kidd was inducted into the Naismith Memorial Basketball Hall of Fame.

VINCE CARTER

8X NBA ALL-STAR

1X ALL-NBA SECOND TEAM

NBA ROOKIE OF THE YEAR (1999)

BORN
January 26, 1977
Daytona Beach, Florida, U.S.

POSITION
Shooting guard / small forward

NBA DRAFT
1998 / round: 1 / pick: 5

Vince Carter was one of the best three-point shooters and scorers in NBA history. He was famous for his amazing dunks and high-flying plays. They earned him the nicknames "Vinsanity" and "Half Man, Half Amazing."

In high school, Vince was an All-American star. He played college basketball at North Carolina for three years. He helped his team reach the Final Four twice.

"Vince, get ready to stay after practice," his coach told him after practice one day. "We're working on your jumper. When you can hit shots from anywhere, you'll be unstoppable in the NBA."

Vince nodded. "Let's do it. I want to be the best, Coach. I'll do whatever it takes."

The Golden State Warriors picked Vince with the fifth overall pick in the 1998 NBA Draft. But they traded him to the Toronto Raptors immediately.

When he arrived in Toronto, veteran teammate Doug Christie gave him some advice.

"Rookie, listen up," Christie said. "The NBA is different. These guys are bigger, stronger, smarter. You're gonna have to adapt fast."

Vince nodded. "I hear you. But I plan to give them something they've never seen before."

In Toronto, he quickly became a star. He won the 1999 NBA Rookie of the Year Award by averaging 18.3 points per game and making amazing dunks. He played for the Raptors from 1998 to 2004 and was a fan favorite.

Nicknamed "Vinsanity," Vince was a five-time All-Star with the Raptors. He even won the 2000 Slam Dunk Contest. His famous 360 windmill dunk is still one of the most talked-about dunks in NBA history.

In 2004, Vince asked to be traded because the Raptors were rebuilding. So, they traded him to the New Jersey Nets.

When the Nets got Vince, fans didn't know what to expect. His new teammate, Jason Kidd, made sure to set the tone at his first practice.

"Alright, Vinsanity, let's see what you got," Kidd said with a grin. "We know you can dunk, but can you run with us?"

Vince grinned. "Run with you? Man, I'll fly past you."

Richard Jefferson, standing nearby, laughed. "I don't know, Vince. We move fast here. This ain't Toronto. You gotta keep up."

Vince took the challenge. He quickly became a key player for the Nets. He averaged 27.5 points, 5.9 rebounds, and 4.7 assists per game in his first season. Every night, he put on a show.

For the next five seasons, Vince was the face of the Nets. He teamed up with Kidd and Jefferson to form a great trio.

In every season with the Nets, he averaged more than 20 points per game. His teammates respected him, and the fans loved him.

As a Net, he played 374 games, averaging 23.6 points, 5.8 rebounds, and 4.7 assists. He led the team to the playoffs three times, reaching the Eastern Conference Semifinals twice. He also played in three All-Star games for the Nets.

In 2009, the Nets traded Vince to the Orlando Magic. He played for four more teams before retiring.

Vince retired with the record for the most game-winning three-point buzzer-beaters in NBA history. He also helped Team USA win a gold medal in the 2000 Summer Olympics.

In 2024, Vince Carter was inducted into the Naismith Memorial Basketball Hall of Fame.

BROOK LOPEZ

NBA CHAMPION (2021)

NBA CUP CHAMPION (2024)

1X NBA ALL-STAR

1X NBA ALL-DEFENSIVE FIRST TEAM

BORN
April 1, 1988
Los Angeles, California, U.S.

POSITION
Center

NBA DRAFT
2008 / round: 1 / pick: 10

For many years, Brook Lopez was one of the most important players for the Brooklyn Nets. People even called him "Mr. Nets."

Brook was always meant to be a great shooter. He had to be. His older brothers also played college basketball. They were taller than him and his twin brother, Robin.

The four brothers played some wild basketball games growing up. Brook had to learn how to shoot from far away so he could score over them.

One day, Robin nudged Brook as they sat on the grass, catching their breath after a tough game.

"You know you only hit that last shot because I slipped, right?" Robin said, laughing.

Brook laughed. "You slipped because I faked you out so badly. It's called skill, little bro."

Robin rolled his eyes. "We're twins. I'm not your 'little bro.'"

Their older brother, Alex, walked by and shook his head.

"You two argue more than you actually play. But Brook, you really are getting better at shooting. You've got a nice touch."

Brook grinned. "Thanks. I have to, or else I'll never score against you guys."

Brook played college basketball for two seasons at Stanford University. He played so well in the 2007-08 season that he was named to the First Team All-Pac 10 and the Third Team All-American. After that season, he decided to enter the 2008 NBA Draft.

The night before the draft, Brook and Robin sat in their room, feeling the weight of what was about to happen.

"You think we'll end up on the same team?" Robin asked.

Brook shook his head. "Probably not. But wherever we go, we just gotta show them what the Lopez twins can do."

Robin leaned back in his chair.

"Yeah. Still, it'd be cool to play together again."

Brook smiled. "Maybe someday."

The New Jersey Nets picked Brook with the 10th overall pick in the draft. Robin was picked 15th by the Phoenix Suns.

As a rookie, Brook played well right away. He started for the Nets and averaged 13.0 points, 8.1 rebounds, and shot 53 percent from the field. He played so well that he made the NBA All-Rookie First Team.

When the Nets traded Vince Carter that season, Brook became one of the team's top players. In his second season, he averaged 18.8 points per game.

One day after practice, coach Lawrence Frank called him over.

"Brook, you're gonna be one of the guys we build around," Frank said.

Brook raised an eyebrow. "Really? That fast?"

Frank nodded. "You've got the skills, and you've got the mindset. But now, you have to step up and be a leader."

Brook took a deep breath. "I'm ready for it."

Brook played nine seasons and 562 games for the Nets. He averaged 18.6 points, 7.1 rebounds, and 1.7 blocks per game. He is the team's all-time leader in blocks with 972 and ranks third in rebounds with 4,005.

In his last game as a Net, he scored 25 points against the Boston Celtics. That game made him the Nets' all-time leading scorer with 10,444 points.

In 2017, Brook was traded to the Los Angeles Lakers. Later, he joined the Milwaukee Bucks, where he won an NBA championship in 2021.

JOE JOHNSON

7X NBA ALL-STAR

1X ALL-NBA THIRD TEAM

NBA ALL-ROOKIE SECOND TEAM

BORN
June 29, 1981
Little Rock, Arkansas, U.S.

POSITION
Shooting guard / small forward

NBA DRAFT
2001 / round: 1 / pick: 10

Joe Johnson was one of the best scorers of his time. He could shoot from deep, drive to the basket, and score in almost any situation. People called him "Iso Joe" because he was great at one-on-one plays.

In high school, Joe's talent made it clear he had a future in basketball. He led his team to a state championship and was named Arkansas Mr. Basketball.

One afternoon after practice, Joe's coach pulled him aside.

"Joe, you ever think about what comes after high school?" his coach asked.

"Yeah. College. And then, hopefully, the league."

The coach nodded and smiled. "You've got the skills. But I want you to work like you're already there. Every rep, every shot, every game. Treat it like it's the NBA Finals."

Joe took a deep breath. "I will. I won't waste any opportunity, Coach."

Joe played college basketball at the University of Arkansas. He helped his team win a championship. He also earned honorable mention All-American honors.

In the 2001 NBA Draft, the Boston Celtics picked Joe with the 10th overall pick.

As a rookie, Joe averaged 7.5 points in 77 games. After 48 games, the Celtics traded him to the Phoenix Suns, where he played for three seasons.

The day after the trade, Suns coach Frank Johnson called him.

"Joe, I know getting traded as a rookie isn't easy," Coach Johnson said.

Joe sighed. "Yeah, I wasn't expecting it. Thought I had more time to prove myself."

"You do. Here, with us," Coach said. "We traded for you because we believe in you. Just be ready to work."

Joe nodded. "I will be."

In his third season, Joe started putting up big numbers, averaging 16.7 points, 4.7 rebounds, and 4.4 assists per game. That kind of play made him an All-Star.

Joe joined the Atlanta Hawks in 2005. In his first five seasons with Atlanta, he averaged 22.0 points, 4.3 rebounds, and 5.5 assists per game.

In 2011, he led the Hawks to the second round of the playoffs. They played six tough games against the top-seeded Chicago Bulls.

Before the 2012–13 season, the Hawks traded Joe to the Brooklyn Nets.

With the Nets, Joe helped the team make the playoffs three times. In 2014, he made his seventh All-Star appearance. Joe led the Nets to the second round, but they lost to the Miami Heat in five games.

After that series, Joe sat in the locker room, staring at the floor.

Coach Jason Kidd walked over. "Tough loss, huh?"

Joe exhaled. "Yeah. It felt like we were close."

Kidd nodded. "We were. But you know what? You showed why they call you Iso Joe. Keep playing like that, and we'll be back."

Joe looked up and nodded. "Yeah. We'll be back."

After 3.5 seasons with the Nets, Joe signed with the Miami Heat in 2016.

Joe played 18 seasons for seven teams. In 1,277 regular-season games, he averaged 16.0 points, 4.0 rebounds, and 3.9 assists. He retired as one of only 50 NBA players to score 20,000 career points.

KEVIN DURANT

2X NBA CHAMPION (2017, 2018)

2X NBA FINALS MVP

14X NBA ALL-STAR

6X ALL-NBA FIRST TEAM

BORN
September 29, 1988
Washington, D.C., U.S.

POSITION
Power forward /
Small forward

NBA DRAFT
2007 / round: 1 / pick: 2

Kevin Durant is considered one of the best basketball players in the world. But his journey started with some challenges.

When Kevin was in middle school, he was unusually tall for his age. He was already six feet. Some kids made fun of him for being so tall. As he walked into class, he heard the familiar whispers.

"Look, it's the giant!" one kid snickered.

Kevin slumped into his seat, trying to make himself smaller. Later that day, he confided in his grandmother.

"Grandma, why do I have to be so tall? Everyone makes fun of me," Kevin said, his voice cracking.

His grandmother cupped his face in her hands.

"Kevin, your height is a gift. One day, you'll see how it makes you perfect for basketball."

Her words stuck with him, fueling a dream that would soon take shape.

When Kevin was around ten, he told his mom he dreamed of becoming an NBA player. His mom, who was raising two boys alone, did everything she could to help him chase that dream. She made sure he stayed focused and practiced hard, even when times were tough.

In high school, Kevin grew even more. He grew an incredible seven inches to reach 6'9". His skills on the basketball court were just as impressive as his height.

Top Division One colleges wanted him to play for them. Kevin, however, chose the University of Texas Longhorns in Austin. He wanted to make his own path.

As a Longhorn, Kevin dominated the court. He won several awards, including the College Player of the Year.

In 2007, he was drafted second overall by the Seattle SuperSonics, who would later become the Oklahoma City Thunder. He quickly proved his talent by winning the NBA Rookie of the Year Award.

After playing nine seasons with the Thunder, Kevin made a huge decision that shocked the NBA. He joined the Golden State Warriors in 2016. Some people criticized him for this, but Kevin knew what he was doing. It turned out to be a winning choice.

In June 2017, Kevin led the Warriors to victory in the NBA Finals against LeBron James and the Cleveland Cavaliers. His incredible scoring earned him the Finals MVP award.

The next year, the Warriors faced the Cavaliers again in the Finals. They defeated them again, and Kevin won his second straight Finals MVP.

In 2019, Kevin Durant left the Golden State Warriors and joined the Brooklyn Nets. But he didn't play at all during the 2019-20 season because he was injured.

The Nets also added six-time All-Star and two-time All-NBA point guard Kyrie Irving. Later, they traded for former MVP James Harden from the Houston Rockets.

With Kevin, Kyrie, and James, the Nets had a superstar trio called the "Big Three." In 2021, they made the playoffs for the third straight year.

But the three stars only played 16 games together. They didn't dominate the way people expected. After three seasons, Kevin was traded to the Phoenix Suns in 2023.

With the Nets, he averaged 29.0 points, 7.1 rebounds, 5.8 assists, and 1.2 blocks per game.

Through it all, Kevin Durant has shown that hard work and determination can turn a tall dream into an amazing reality.

CHAPTER THREE QUIZ

1. What was Julius Erving's nickname?

a. Dr. J

b. Big J

c. The Machine

d. Big Shot

2. What skill was Julius Erving famous for?

a. Sprinting and changing directions quickly

b. Leaping ability

c. Making no-look passes

d. Acrobatic slam dunks

3. Which college did Julius Erving play for?

a. Michigan State

b. University of Massachusetts

c. Oberlin College

d. University of Miami

4. Which year did Julius Erving win the NBA MVP award?

a. 1981

b. 1983

c. 1985

d. 1990

5. Which year was Julius Erving inducted into the Basketball Hall of Fame?

a. 1993

b. 1995

c. 1997

d. 1999

6. What year did the Nets draft Buck Williams?

a. 1970

b. 1975

c. 1981

d. 1988

7. What was Buck Williams mostly famous for?

a. His crossover

b. His dribble

c. His dunk

d. His rebounds

8. What year was Buck Williams named the NBA Rookie of the Year?

a. 1976

b. 1978

c. 1980

d. 1982

9. How many times was Buck Williams an All-Star?

a. 1

b. 2

c. 3

d. 4

10. Which team did Buck Williams join in 1989?

a. Portland Trail Blazers

b. Washington Bullets

c. Chicago Bulls

d. New York Knicks

11. Which country was Dražen Petrović from?

a. Greece

b. Italy

c. Croatia

d. Belgium

12. Which team selected Dražen Petrović in the 1986 NBA Draft?

a. Los Angeles Lakers

b. Oklahoma City Thunder

c. Charlotte Hornets

d. Portland Trail Blazers

13. Which year was Dražen Petrović traded to the Nets?

a. 1989

b. 1991

c. 1993

d. 1995

14. What was Dražen Petrović most famous for?

a. His powerful jumps

b. His strong blocks

c. His three-pointers

d. His leadership on the court

15. How many times was Dražen Petrović named the Croatian Sportsman of the Year?

a. 1

b. 2

c. 3

d. 4

16. How many seasons did Jason Kidd play for the Nets?

a. 7 seasons

b. 8 seasons

c. 9 seasons

d. 10 seasons

17. Which college did Jason Kidd play for?

a. University of North Carolina

b. University of Kentucky

c. Texas A&M

d. University of California, Berkeley

18. What position did Jason Kidd play?

a. Center

b. Power forward

c. Small forward

d. Point guard

19. How many times was Jason Kidd an All-Star?

a. 10

b. 12

c. 14

d. 16

20. How many rebounds did Jason Kidd catch in his career?

a. 2,781 rebounds

b. 3,662 rebounds

c. 4,176 rebounds

d. 5,987 rebounds

21. What was Vince Carter's nickname?

a. Insane Carter

b. Vince the Man

c. Vinsanity

d. Air Vince

22. Which year did Vince Carter win the Slam Dunk Contest?

a. 2000

b. 2001

c. 2002

d. 2003

23. Which team did Vince Carter play for before joining the Nets?

a. Denver Nuggets

b. Los Angeles Lakers

c. San Diego Clippers

d. Toronto Raptors

24. How many games did Vince Carter play with the Nets?

a. 290 games

b. 328 games

c. 374 games

d. 412 games

25. Which year was Vince Carter inducted into the Basketball Hall of Fame?

a. 2022

b. 2023

c. 2024

d. 2025

26. What year did the Nets draft Brook Lopez?

a. 2008

b. 2009

c. 2010

d. 2011

27. What happened to Brook Lopez in his rookie season?

a. He suddenly fainted during a game

b. He was traded to another team

c. He decided to retire from the NBA

d. He made the NBA All-Rookie First Team

28. How many seasons did Brook Lopez play for the Nets?

a. 6 seasons

b. 9 seasons

c. 11 seasons

d. 13 seasons

29. How many times was Brook Lopez an All-Star?

a. 1

b. 2

c. 3

d. 4

30. Which team did Brook Lopez win the NBA Championship with in 2021?

a. Los Angeles Lakers

b. Brooklyn Nets

c. Milwaukee Bucks

d. Orlando Magic

31. How did Joe Johnson get his nickname "Iso Joe?"

a. He liked spending time alone

b. He was great at one-on-one plays

c. He did not like passing the ball to his teammates

d. He loved drinking isotonic drinks during games

32. What title did Joe Johnson win in high school?

a. Player of the Year

b. Arkansas Most Valuable Player

c. Arkansas Mr. Basketball

d. Best Offensive Player of the Year

33. How many teams did Joe Johnson play for during his 18 year NBA career?

a. 3

b. 5

c. 7

d. 9

34. How many times was Joe Johnson an All-Star?

a. 7

b. 8

c. 9

d. 10

35. Why was Kevin Durant made fun of in middle school?

a. He kept failing his exams

b. He spoke with a stutter

c. He was not good at sports

d. He was taller than everyone else

36. **Which team drafted Kevin Durant in 2007?**

a. Seattle SuperSonics

b. Golden State Warriors

c. Los Angeles Clippers

d. Dallas Mavericks

37. **What award did Kevin Durant win in his rookie year?**

a. NBA Most Valuable Player Award

b. NBA Rookie of the Year Award

c. NBA Player of the Week Award

d. NBA Defensive Player of the Year Award

38. **How many seasons did Kevin Durant play for the Nets?**

a. 3 seasons

b. 4 seasons

c. 5 seasons

d. 6 seasons

Quiz Answers

1. Dr. J **2.** Acrobatic slam dunks **3.** University of Massachusetts **4.** 1981 **5.** 1993 **6.** 1981 **7.** His rebounds **8.** 1982 **9.** 3 All-Star **10.** Portland Trail Blazers **11.** Croatia **12.** Portland Trail Blazers **13.** 1991 **14.** His three-pointers **15.** 2 times **16.** 7 seasons **17.** University of California, Berkeley **18.** Point guard **19.** 10 All-Star **20.** 3,662 rebounds **21.** Vinsanity **22.** 2000 **23.** Toronto Raptors **24.** 374 games **25.** 2024 **26.** 2008 **27.** He made the NBA All-Rookie First Team **28.** 9 seasons **29.** 1 All-Star **30.** Milwaukee Bucks **31.** He was great at one-on-one plays **32.** Arkansas Mr. Basketball **33.** 7 teams **34.** 7 All-Star **35.** He was taller than everyone else **36.** Seattle SuperSonics **37.** NBA Rookie of the Year Award **38.** 3 seasons

CHAPTER FOUR

Coaches And Their Impact

Behind every great basketball team is a visionary coach who inspires players and creates a winning culture. During the Brooklyn Nets' long history, many legendary coaches have guided the team through wins and challenges from the sidelines.

Kevin Loughery was the head coach of the Brooklyn Nets from 1973 to 1980. He helped them win two ABA championships in three seasons. During that time, Loughery had Julius "Dr. J" Erving on the team. He was one of the best players ever.

Before becoming a coach, Loughery was a basketball player who spent 11 seasons in the NBA. He played for the Detroit Pistons, Baltimore Bullets, and Philadelphia 76ers. He started his coaching career with the 76ers as a player-coach in 1973.

When Loughery became the Nets' coach, he expected his players to work hard. He knew the game well and was a strong leader. The players respected him because he had been on the court just like them.

Under Loughery, the Nets became a great team in the late 1970s. He let Dr. J take over games with his amazing dunks, scoring, and defense. Under Loughery, the Nets became one of the most exciting teams in basketball.

After the ABA ended and the Nets joined the NBA, Loughery stayed as their coach for their first five seasons in the league.

Loughery was a fiery and passionate coach. He always wanted his players to give their best effort. He was also known for arguing with referees and getting a lot of technical fouls. He has one of the most technical fouls in NBA history.

After coaching the Nets for eight seasons, Loughery was fired in the middle of the 1980-81 season. He later coached the Atlanta Hawks, Chicago Bulls, Washington Bullets, and Miami Heat.

During his time in Brooklyn, Loughery won 297 games and lost 318. He also led the team to 21 playoff wins. His years with the Nets were filled with great moments and big accomplishments.

Another important coach in Brooklyn Nets history was Byron Scott. He coached the team for 3.5 seasons, from 2000 to 2004.

The Nets hadn't reached the NBA Finals or won a division title before Scott became coach. During his time with the team, he led the Nets to the NBA Finals in back-to-back seasons, 2002 and 2003.

When Scott first joined the team, the Nets performed poorly in his first year, winning just 26 games. However, the team would improve in the next season with the arrival of star point guard Jason Kidd.

In the 2001-2002 season, the team set a franchise record with 52 wins and won the Atlantic Division title. This remarkable turnaround was largely due to Jason Kidd and Scott's effective coaching.

An important game during Scott's tenure was Game 5 of the 2002 Eastern Conference Finals against the Boston Celtics.

The series was tied 2-2, and the Nets needed a win to gain momentum. They secured a decisive victory and went on to win the series, earning their first trip to the NBA Finals.

Scott was fired during the 2003-04 season. He won 149 regular-season games with the team. After that, he coached the New Orleans Hornets, Cleveland Cavaliers, and Los Angeles Lakers. In 2008, he was named NBA Coach of the Year while coaching the New Orleans Hornets.

Even though Scott did not win a championship with the Nets, he greatly impacted the team. He was known for his ability to transform the Nets into a competitive team.

CHAPTER FOUR QUIZ

1. Which year was Kevin Loughery made the Nets' coach?

a. 1968

b. 1973

c. 1977

d. 1986

2. How many seasons did Kevin Loughery coach the Nets?

a. 4 seasons

b. 6 seasons

c. 8 seasons

d. 10 seasons

3. How many regular-season games did Kevin Loughery win with the Nets?

a. 316 games

b. 410 games

c. 610 games

d. 728 games

4. How many ABA Championships did the Nets win with Kevin Loughery?

a. 1

b. 2

c. 3

d. 4

5. Which year was Byron Scott made the Nets' coach?

a. 2000

b. 2001

c. 2002

d. 2003

6. How many times did the Nets reach the NBA Finals with Byron Scott?

a. 1

b. 2

c. 3

d. 4

7. How many regular-season games did Byron Scott win with the Nets?

a. 96 games

b. 123 games

c. 149 games

d. 205 games

Quiz Answers

1. 1973 **2.** 8 seasons **3.** 297 games **4.** 2 ABA Championships **5.** 2000 **6.** 2 NBA Finals **7.** 149 games

CHAPTER FIVE
Memorable Moments in Nets' History

The Brooklyn Nets have had some amazing moments that fans will never forget. From winning the ABA Championship in 1974 to special moments like becoming back-to-back Eastern Conference Champions, here are four exciting and unforgettable moments in Nets history.

1974 ABA CHAMPIONSHIP VICTORY

The arena buzzed with excitement as the New York Nets stepped onto the court for Game 5 of the 1974 ABA Finals. The championship was within reach, but they had to finish off the Utah Stars first. Julius "Dr. J" Erving looked around at his teammates.

"This is it, guys," he said, bouncing the ball once before passing it to Brian Taylor. "Forty-eight minutes to make history."

Billy Paultz, the big center nicknamed "The Whopper," clapped his hands. "Let's shut them down. No mercy."

The referee blew his whistle, and the game began.

From the start, Dr. J was unstoppable. He soared through the air for layups, his afro bouncing as he twisted past defenders.

He hit jump shots, dished out passes, and grabbed rebounds like the ball belonged to him. The Utah Stars tried to slow him down, but nothing worked.

"Somebody stop that man!" a Utah player yelled after another one of Erving's smooth moves.

By halftime, the Nets had built a slim lead, but the Stars weren't giving up. In the third quarter, Utah's Ron Boone hit back-to-back shots. Their big man, Zelmo Beaty, powered through for tough baskets.

"We can't let them get comfortable," Taylor told Erving during a timeout.

Erving nodded. "Time to turn it up."

The fourth quarter belonged to the Nets. Dr. J spun past defenders for a dunk that shook the rim, and Paultz muscled inside for a layup.

With less than a minute left, the fans at Nassau Coliseum were on their feet. The Nets were up by ten. The clock ticked down. 10 seconds, 9, 8…

Paultz grabbed the final rebound and held the ball as the buzzer sounded. The Nets had won their first ABA Championship!

"We did it!" Taylor shouted, throwing his arms around Dr. J.

The team huddled in the center of the court, jumping and celebrating. Dr. J was named the Most Valuable Player of the ABA playoffs. The Nets were now champions, their names forever etched in basketball history.

SECOND ABA CHAMPIONSHIP VICTORY (1976)

The locker room was quiet. It was May 13, 1976. The New York Nets were leading the 1976 ABA Championship series. But, Game 6 against the Denver Nuggets would not be easy. The Nuggets were tough, and everyone in the arena knew it.

The Nuggets came out firing, hitting shots from everywhere. Their star, David Thompson, soared for layups, and Dan Issel powered his way inside.

By the second quarter, the Nets were in trouble. The scoreboard glowed: Denver 28, New York 23.

Coach Kevin Loughery called a timeout.

"Alright, listen up," he said, looking every player in the eye. "They're throwing everything at us, but we're not done. And we let Doc do what he does best."

Dr. J nodded. "Let's go get this."

The Nets came back to life. Erving glided through defenders for a layup. Then he hit a jumper. Brian Taylor drilled a three-pointer. The defense tightened, forcing turnovers.

As they sat on the bench, Taylor nudged Erving.

"Are you planning on taking over now, or should we wait until the last second?"

Erving grinned. "Stick around. I have a plan."

The second half was a battle. The Nets trailed 80-58 with 16 minutes remaining.

The teams traded baskets, and the lead swung back and forth. With under a minute left, the Nets clung to a six-point lead.

Denver had the ball. The crowd roared as Thompson drove to the basket, but Erving leaped up and swatted the shot away.

The Nets bench exploded. Moments later, the buzzer sounded. The final score was 112-106. The Nets had won their second ABA Championship.

Taylor pumped his fist. "ABA champions, again!"

The team celebrated at center court, confetti falling all around them. As he held the championship trophy, Erving smiled.

"This one's for all of us," he said. "Champions forever."

1984 NBA PLAYOFF SERIES WIN

The New Jersey Nets huddled together in the locker room, their hearts pounding. It was April 26, 1984. They were about to play Game 5 of their first-round playoff series against the Philadelphia 76ers.

The 76ers were the defending champion. Meanwhile, the Nets had finished in fourth place in the Atlantic Division.

Nobody expected the Nets to be in the playoffs. Nobody thought they could win. But now, with one more victory, they could pull off one of the biggest upsets in NBA history.

Buck Williams, the team's leader, stood up and looked around at his teammates.

"They think we can't win in Philly for the third time in the series. Let's prove them wrong."

The players nodded, then jogged onto the court at the Spectrum in Philadelphia. The crowd was loud, booing the Nets and chanting for their Sixers.

From the start, it was a battle. Julius Erving was now playing for the Sixers. He drove to the basket for a dunk. Moses Malone powered inside for tough layups. But, the Nets answered back with points from Otis Birdsong and Micheal Richardson.

At halftime, the game was tight. The 76ers were leading 53-50.

Coach Stan Albeck gathered the players.

"You see that scoreboard? You see how they're sweating? They know we are not giving up. Keep pushing."

The third quarter was a fight. The Sixers started pulling away and building a lead. The crowd roared as they scored another long jumper.

Richardson turned to Williams. "We gotta hit back, Buck."

Williams nodded. "Let's go."

The Nets locked in on defense. Williams grabbed rebound after rebound, while Richardson drove through defenders for tough layups. Birdsong nailed a jumper. Slowly, the lead shrank.

With two minutes left, the Nets had taken the lead by one. The crowd grew tense. The Sixers weren't used to losing like this.

The Nets worked the ball around. With 20 seconds left, Richardson found Albert King in the corner. King faked, took one dribble, and pulled up.

Swish!

The Nets bench jumped to their feet. The lead was three.

The Sixers had one last shot, but the Nets' defense held strong. When the final buzzer sounded, it was over. The Nets had won Game 5 101-98.

The Nets had won the series 3-2, their first-ever NBA playoff series victory.

Williams grabbed Richardson. "We did it!"

Richardson grinned. "And they never saw it coming."

The Nets walked off the court, heads held high, knowing they had just made history.

2003 EASTERN CONFERENCE CHAMPIONSHIP

The New Jersey Nets were one win away from the NBA Finals, but they weren't celebrating yet. They still had to get past the Detroit Pistons in Game 4 of the Eastern Conference Finals.

If they win this game, they will head to the Finals for the second straight year. Lose, and they will have to fly back to Detroit for another battle.

In the locker room before the game, Jason Kidd stood up and looked around at his teammates.

"We don't give them a chance," he said. "We finish it tonight."

Kenyon Martin nodded. "I like the sound of that."

Richard Jefferson grinned. "Let's put on a show."

From the opening tip, the Nets played with energy. Kidd zipped passes to teammates, setting up easy baskets.

The Pistons weren't going down without a fight. But every time the Pistons scored, the Nets answered right back.

At halftime, the Nets were in control, leading by 9 points.

In the third quarter, Detroit made a run. They grabbed rebounds and threw down dunks. The lead shrank to six points with 9:29 minutes to play.

Kidd pulled his team together. "We do not panic," he said. "We know what we gotta do."

The Nets locked in. With just a few minutes left, Kidd drove to the hoop, drew the defense, and tossed a perfect alley-oop to Martin.

Martin caught it in mid-air and slammed it home. The arena erupted.

With the clock ticking down, the Pistons tried to fight back, but the Nets wouldn't let them. When the final buzzer sounded, the scoreboard told the story: Nets 102, Pistons 82.

They had done it. Back-to-back Eastern Conference Champions. Now, the NBA Finals awaited.

CHAPTER FIVE QUIZ

1. Which team did the Nets defeat in the 1974 ABA Finals?

a. New York Knicks

b. San Antonio Spurs

c. Dallas Mavericks

d. Utah Stars

2. Which player was named the Most Valuable Player of the 1974 ABA playoffs?

a. Billy Paultz

b. Julius Erving

c. Brian Taylor

d. Ron Boone

3. Which team did the Nets defeat in the 1976 ABA Championship?

a. Denver Nuggets

b. Los Angeles Lakers

c. Boston Celtics

d. Detroit Pistons

4. What was the final score of Game 6 in the 1976 ABA Championship?

a. Nets won 83-79

b. Nets won 93-89

c. Nets won 104-95

d. Nets won 112-106

5. What was the final score of Game 5 against the 76ers in the 1984 playoffs?

a. Nets won 99-98

b. Nets won 101-98

c. Nets won 110-102

d. Nets won 131-129

6. Which player led the Nets to victory at the 2003 Eastern Conference Finals?

a. Jason Kidd

b. Kevin Durant

c. Joe Johnson

d. Vince Carter

Quiz Answers

1. Utah Stars **2.** Julius Erving **3.** Denver Nuggets **4.** Nets won 112-106 **5.** Nets won 101-98 **6.** Jason Kidd

CHAPTER SIX
Fun Facts and Trivia!

The Brooklyn Nets were the first major sports team in Brooklyn since the Dodgers left in 1957.

When they joined the ABA in 1967, they were called the New Jersey Americans and wore red and white uniforms.

The Nets have retired the jersey numbers of many iconic players. Some of the most iconic Nets numbers to have been retired include #3 (Dražen Petrović), #5 (Jason Kidd), and #32 (Julius Erving).

After moving to Brooklyn, the team introduced a superhero mascot named BrooklyKnight on November 3, 2012.

However, fans didn't like it, saying it looked too scary for kids and not funny enough. The team retired BrooklyKnight after two years.

At first, the NBA didn't want the Nets to use black and white when they moved to Brooklyn. Many teams had been denied similar requests.

But Jay-Z, who owned a small part of the team, helped make it happen. He designed the logo, chose the colors, and convinced the NBA to approve the change.

Kyrie Irving has scored the most points for the Nets in a game, with 60 points against the Magic on March 15, 2022.

In 1994, the New Jersey Nets almost became the New Jersey Swamp Dragons. They even designed a logo. The NBA approved the name change, but at the last moment, the Nets changed their minds and voted against it.

The New Jersey Nets wanted to draft Kobe Bryant with the eighth pick in 1996. But Kobe said he would play in Italy if they picked him. So, the Nets chose Kerry Kittles instead. Many fans see this as a missed chance to get one of the greatest players ever.

The New Jersey Nets picked Kyle Korver 51st in the 2003 draft but had no room for him. Their team was already led by Jason Kidd, Richard Jefferson, and Kenyon Martin. So, they sold Korver's rights to the 76ers.

The money helped pay for Summer League fees and even bought a copy machine. Korver used this as motivation and became one of the best three-point shooters of the 2010s.

No one could have guessed Korver would become a great shooter in 2003. But trading him for a copy machine is still one of the strangest deals in NBA history.

In 2010, the Nets had the worst attendance in the NBA. On February 10, fewer than 1,000 fans showed up, setting a new low. Things were so bad that the team even offered free New Jersey state tax services to people who went to games.

In 1994, the Nets had two starters in the All-Star Game. Kenny Anderson and Derrick Coleman became the first Nets players to start in an All-Star Game.

The all-time franchise leader in points is Brook Lopez, after scoring 10,444 points. He scored four points more than second-placed Buck Williams. Lopez averaged 18.7 points per game for the Nets.

HERE ARE MORE QUESTIONS TO TEST YOUR KNOWLEDGE OF THE NETS!

1. What are the official team colors of the Nets?

a. Blue, Silver, and White

b. Red, White, and Blue

c. Black and White

d. Green, Black, and Gold

2. Who was the Nets' head coach before Jordi Fernández?

a. Jacque Vaughn

b. Steve Nash

c. Kenny Atkinson

d. Lionel Hollins

3. Who was the first-ever head coach of the Brooklyn Nets?

a. P.J. Carlesimo

b. Avery Johnson

c. Jason Kidd

d. Lionel Hollins

4. Which Nets player won the Rookie of the Year in 1991?

a. Buck Williams

b. Sam Bowie

c. Mookie Blaylock

d. Derrick Coleman

5. What number did Jason Kidd wear for the Nets?

a. 5

b. 23

c. 48

d. 57

6. What year did the Nets retire Jason Kidd's number?

a. 2010

b. 2011

c. 2012

d. 2013

7. Which team did the Nets lose to in the first round of the 2023 NBA Playoffs?

a. Miami Heat

b. Philadelphia 76ers

c. Boston Celtics

d. Milwaukee Bucks

8. Who led the Nets in scoring during the 2012-13 season, their first in Brooklyn?

a. Deron Williams

b. Gerald Wallace

c. Brook Lopez

d. Joe Johnson

9. Who was the New Jersey Nets' first All-Star?

a. Buck Williams

b. Deron Williams

c. Kevin Garnett

d. Brook Lopez

10. What pick was Brook Lopez in the 2008 NBA Draft?

a. 3rd

b. 8th

c. 12th

d. 15th

11. Which team did the Nets trade Kyrie Irving to in 2023?

a. Phoenix Suns

b. Golden State Warriors

c. Dallas Mavericks

d. Utah Jazz

12. What is the name of the Nets' G-League affiliate?

a. Brooklyn Fire

b. Long Island Nets

c. The Brooklyn Charge

d. Brooklyn Blue Coats

13. In what year did the Nets first have three players in the All-Star Game?

a. 1995

b. 2000

c. 2006

d. 2021

ABOUT THE AUTHOR

John Stevenson is a Michigan-based author of children's sports books. He is the father of two children, James and Tracy. When not writing new books, John can be found playing sports with his family or going on road trips. Through his books, John hopes to empower young readers and spark their imagination.

ENJOYED THE BOOK?

I'd really appreciate it if you could leave a review on Amazon. The number of reviews a book receives helps more people discover it. Even a short review can make a big difference, allowing me to keep doing what I love. Thank you in advance!

Trivia Answers

1. Black and White **2.** Jacque Vaughn **3.** Avery Johnson **4.** Derrick Coleman **5.** 5 **6.** 2013 **7.** Philadelphia 76ers **8.** Brook Lopez **9.** Buck Williams **10.** 8th **11.** Dallas Mavericks **12.** Long Island Nets **13.** 2021